CAMEL

by Caroline Arnold

Photographs by Richard Hewett

MORROW JUNIOR BOOKS · NEW YORK

PHOTO CREDITS
Permission to use the following photographs is gratefully acknowledged: Arthur Arnold, pages 44, 45, 46–47; Zoological Society of San Diego, page 16 (top right).

The text type is 12 point Galliard.

Library of Congress Cataloging-in-Publication Data. Arnold, Caroline. Camel / by Caroline Arnold ; photographs by Richard Hewett.   p.   cm. Summary: Discusses the habitats, physical characteristics, and behavior of the two kinds of camels. ISBN 0-688-09498-8 (trade).—ISBN 0-688-09499-6 (library)
1. Camels—Juvenile literature.   [1. Camels.]   I. Hewett, Richard, ill.   II. Title.
QL737.U54A75   1992 599.73′6—dc20   91-26805   CIP   AC

ACKNOWLEDGMENTS

We are grateful to the staff of Wildlife Safari in Winston, Oregon, for their help on this project and for allowing us to photograph the camels in the park. We also thank the Los Angeles Zoo and the Los Angeles County Museum of Natural History for their assistance. And, as always, we thank our editor, Andrea Curley, for her continued enthusiastic support.

Pressed snugly against his mother's side, the one-week-old baby camel sniffed the moist morning air. Well protected by a coat of short, curly hair, the young camel stayed warm and dry even in the light spring rain. When the weather turned hot later, his coat would protect him from the heat as well.

The baby camel was born at a wildlife park in southern Oregon, where he lives with his mother, Trina, his father, Felix, and another male camel called Oscar. The keepers at the park had named the baby camel Mguu, an African name referring to his long, skinny legs. On his back Mguu had two tiny bulges that would gradually grow into large humps like those of the other camels.

In the park, Mguu and the other camels roam the forests and hillsides of their enclosure along with other Asian animals such as yaks, small goats called tahrs, and Sika deer. The Oregon landscape is wetter and more wooded than the camels' native home in central Asia. However, they are comfortable in the park, where they have plenty of food, water, and room to roam.

Visitors to the wildlife park can drive through it and observe the animals from inside their vehicles. Like many of the animals that live there, the camels have become so accustomed to people that they hardly pay any attention when someone stops to look at them. Although the camels and other animals in the park may seem quite tame, they must be treated as wild animals, and visitors are instructed not to touch or feed them.

Mguu, his parents, and Oscar are bactrian camels. These two-humped camels are found in Asia in the mountainous desert regions that range from Mongolia, northern China, and the Soviet Union westward to parts of Turkey. Here, camels live on vast, sparsely vegetated plains and in the rocky mountains that border them. As in other deserts, there is little rain, so food and water are scarce.

The name *bactrian* comes from a valley in northern Afghanistan, which in ancient times was called Baktria. It is thought that wild camels were first tamed here more than four thousand years ago. As they still do today, people used the sturdy animals for riding and to carry heavy loads. As such, camels have been essential for trade and transportation for many centuries in desert regions of the world. The name *camel* may be derived from an ancient Middle Eastern word, *gamal,* which means "carrying a burden." Camels are also useful as sources of meat, milk, wool, and leather, and their dried dung can be used as fuel.

9

Bactrian camels.

Today, most bactrian camels are domestic animals; that is, they are bred by people and live and work with them. Although a few herds of wild bactrians live in the Gobi Desert of Mongolia, there are fewer than one thousand of these wild camels left. They are in danger of becoming extinct as towns develop around the waterholes on which they depend. Wild bactrian camels are thinner and have less hair than domestic animals. Mguu and the other camels in the park are from domestic stock.

There are two species of camels: the bactrian, whose scientific name is *Camelus bactrianus,* and the Arabian, whose scientific name is *Camelus dromedarius.* Bactrian camels have shorter legs, heavier bodies, and longer, thicker coats than their one-humped relatives, the Arabian camels. (An Arabian camel actually has a small second hump just behind its shoulders, but this hump is not usually big

Arabian camel.

enough to notice.) Arabian camels are found throughout the Middle East and across the deserts of North Africa.

Both kinds of camels are able to live in places where the climate is extreme and food and water are scarce. In the Gobi Desert, where many bactrian camels live, there is little rainfall and temperatures range from below freezing in winter to 122 degrees Fahrenheit (50 degrees Celsius) in summer. Arabians also live in very hot, dry des-erts, but they do not need to withstand the extremely cold temperatures that bactrians do. But even though the two kinds of camels usually live in some-what different environments, their habits and behavior are similar in many ways. In some places, such as the southern Soviet Union and Syria, both bactrians and Arabians are found and the two kinds of camels sometimes in-terbreed. The offspring is known as a *tulu* and usually has two humps.

All Arabian camels are domestic animals. It is believed that these one-humped camels were originally bred from two-humped camels. No one knows exactly when this occurred, but there is no record of one-humped camels before about six thousand years ago.

Occasionally a domestic camel will escape from its owner or be set free. When a domestic animal goes back to the wild and lives as a wild animal, it is said to be feral. A feral animal is not the same as a wild animal because its origins are from domestic stock. Many herds of feral Arabian camels now live in the vast deserts of central Australia. About one hundred years ago their ancestors were brought to Australia and they adapted easily to the dry land there. Today the camels in Australia number about fifty thousand.

For many years a few feral Arabian camels also roamed the deserts of the southwestern United States. In the 1850s the U.S. government imported some camels and created the Camel Corps. The army used these camels to transport goods to distant forts in the new western states. When the Camel Corps was abandoned at the end of the Civil War, many of the camels were turned loose. They gradually died or were killed. The last "wild" camel was seen in 1941 in California.

The term "dromedary" is sometimes used mistakenly to refer to Arabian camels in general. All kinds of camels can be ridden, but the dromedary is a breed of Arabian specially bred for riding. The word *dromedary* is derived from an ancient Greek word that means "running." In some countries today, camel racing is still a popular sport.

To ride a dromedary or an Arabian camel, one sits in a saddle that is balanced over the single hump. The saddle for a bactrian camel fits between the two humps. Just as a horse must be taught to allow a person on its back, camels must be trained to be riding animals, too. Usually the rider mounts and dismounts when the camel is in a kneeling position.

Dromedaries, which are selected for speed and endurance, are able to gallop 100 miles (161.3 kilometers) in a single day. Camels wearing packs usually travel at about 3 miles (4.8 kilometers) per hour. For them, a typical day's journey is about 25 miles (40.3 kilometers). A group of people and camels traveling together is called a caravan. Caravans may include thousands of camels or just a few.

The camel has played an important role in the history of humankind. In addition to its use as a riding and pack animal, a camel can be hitched to a plow, pull a wagon, or walk a treadmill of a water-pumping machine. In ancient wars the camel was used to transport people, weapons, and supplies.

Upper left, alpaca; upper right, vicuña; lower left, guanaco; lower right, llamas.

All camels belong to the family of animals called camelids. The first camelids lived more than 40 million years ago in North America. Unlike camels today, these animals were only about 12 inches (30 centimeters) tall and had no humps.

Some of the early camelids migrated to South America, where they adapted to life in the high, dry mountains and evolved into what are now guanacos and vicuñas. Today, herds of guanacos can be found throughout the Andes Mountains and on the plains of Argentina. The vicuña, a more delicate animal adapted to life at very high altitudes in the Andes, has long been prized for its fine, silky wool. Once extremely endangered, it is now protected.

About four thousand years ago, people in South America began to domesticate the wild guanacos and developed the animals that are known today as llamas and alpacas. Today most llamas and alpacas are found in Peru. Llamas are strong and surefooted, and people use them as pack animals along narrow mountain trails. Llamas also provide meat, milk, and wool. The smaller alpacas are raised for their warm wool, which is used to make beautiful blankets and clothing.

In North America, early camelids gradually evolved into large, humped animals similar to present-day camels. About a million years ago, during an ice age, some of these North American camels traveled across the ice and land bridge that joined Alaska and Asia at the Bering Strait. They are the ancestors of today's bactrians and Arabians. At the end of this ice age, the climate in North America changed and many animals, including these prehistoric camels, became extinct. About ten thousand years ago, the last North American camels died out, in part perhaps because they were hunted by people.

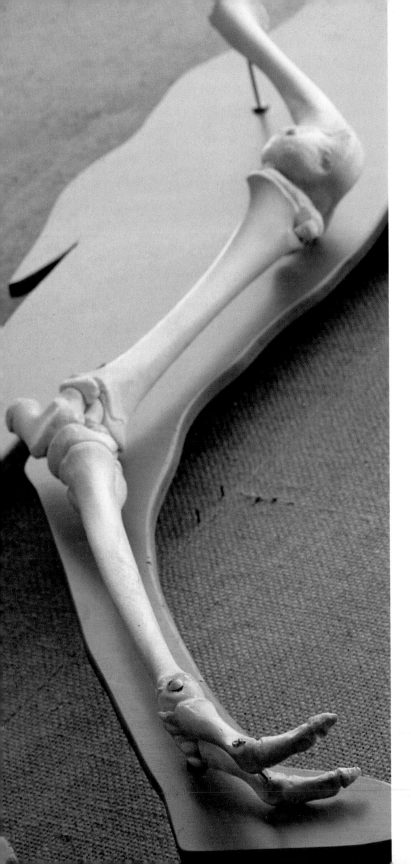

Camel leg and foot bones.

The camelids belong to the large group of even-toed hoofed animals whose scientific name is artiodactyl. This group includes cattle, deer, and many other animals. The camel has two toes on each foot. Although the toenails form small hooves, the camel actually walks on large sole pads on the bottom of its feet. These tough, leathery pads can be as wide as 7 inches (17.9 centimeters), and their broad surface helps prevent the camel from sinking into soft sand or snow.

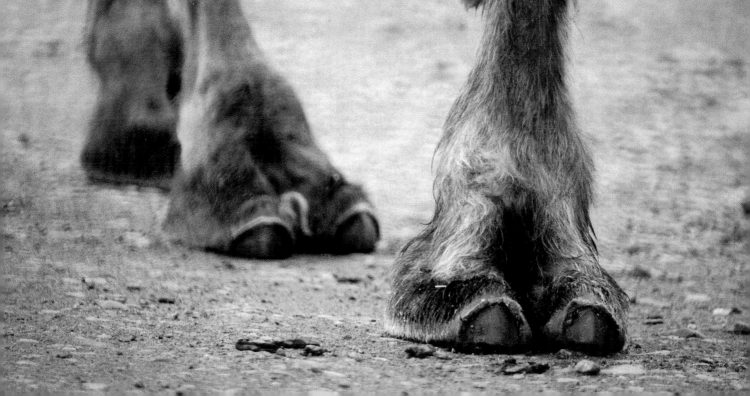

Female bactrian, left; and male bactrian, right.

Camels are among the largest land animals. Measured at the top of his hump, an adult male bactrian camel stands about 7 feet (2.1 meters) tall. In length he is about 10 feet (3 meters) from nose to rump, plus an 18-inch (46.2-centimeter) tail. The average weight for a full-grown male is about 1,200 pounds (545.5 kilograms). Arabians weigh about the same as bactrians, but because of their longer legs they are usually about 6 inches (15.4 centimeters) taller. In both species males are somewhat larger than females.

Another difference between male and female camels is their teeth. Both sexes have the same kinds of teeth for eating, but in the front of the male's mouth some of the teeth are long and sharp. Males use these teeth to bite each other when they fight.

Male bactrian.

In the wild, a strong male camel collects a group, or *harem,* of several females and mates with them. To maintain his position as leader, he must defend his harem against outside males and attacks them with a loud roar. With domestic camels, the males fight with each other for the right to mate with the females in the herd. Camel owners often neuter their males when they are young in order to prevent such fights. Neutered males cannot produce offspring and they are less interested in females.

Because camels are riding animals, people often use the same terms for them as for horses. Male camels are sometimes called *stallions,* females are called *mares,* and babies are called *foals.* More often, however, baby camels are referred to as *calves.*

A female camel begins to breed when she is four or five years old and usually produces a new baby every two years. After mating, the female camel is pregnant for twelve to thirteen months. Most matings and births occur during the wet season, when the weather is neither too hot nor too cold and there is plenty of food.

Usually a female gives birth to a single calf, although sometimes twins are produced. The newborn calf has tiny humps and is covered by a short, woolly coat. It weighs about 80 pounds (36.4 kilograms) and stands about 4 feet (1.2 meters) at the hump.

Like other hoofed animals, the camel baby is well developed at birth. Its eyes are open, and within an hour or so it can stand. The calf's body is small, but its legs are nearly as long as an adult's. Although they are shaky at first, the legs quickly grow strong. Almost from the moment of its birth, the calf must be able to follow its mother and stay with the herd.

Unlike many other animals, a camel mother does not lick her newborn clean. Instead, she lets its wet wool dry in the sun. She watches over her baby carefully, however, and makes sure that it is safe.

During his first weeks, Mguu always stayed close to his mother as she and the other camels moved through the park. Whenever Mguu wanted to get Trina's attention, he called out with short, sheeplike bleats.

As with other mammals, a young camel's first food is its mother's milk. Almost immediately after he stood for the first time, Mguu began to nuzzle under his mother's belly in search of one of her teats. People who keep camels often use their milk, too. Camel milk can be drunk or used to make butter or cheese. Mguu drank Trina's milk until he was three or four months old. After that he began to eat plant foods like the older camels.

Camels are herbivores, or plant eaters. If camels are on their own, they spend eight to twelve hours a day grazing. In places where camels are used as work animals, they are usually turned loose at night to feed on nearby shrubbery or whatever they can find. Although vegetation is sparse in the desert, camels can usually find enough to eat. In the morning the camels almost always return to their owners to get water and salt. Like most animals, camels need some salt in their diet. At the wildlife park where Mguu lives, blocks of salt are placed where the animals can lick them whenever they want.

Camels can get most of the water they need from their food if it is moist, and in cool weather a camel can go for six months without drinking. Even in extremely hot weather, camels can get along with little water, going for a week or more without a drink.

A split upper lip makes it possible for camels to get their teeth close to the ground so they can eat short grass when it is available. Camels are not fussy and will eat almost any vegetation, including sharp twigs, thornbushes, salt bushes, and other plants that grow in the dry regions where they normally live. Tough skin on the inside of a camel's mouth protects it from these rough foods. Usually camels eat only some of what they find, nibbling a little from each plant before moving on. This helps the plants to grow in the same way that pruning helps plants to thrive in a garden.

Although the camels in the wildlife park eat lush new grass in the spring, their diet for most of the year is hay, which is provided for them in large bins. Until Mguu was old enough to eat solid food, he waited patiently at Trina's feet whenever she stopped to nibble some hay. Adult camels like Trina, Oscar, and Felix that live in a zoo or wildlife park normally eat about 8 pounds (3.6 kilograms) of food each day. Working camels, however, need much more. They can eat up to 44 pounds (20 kilograms) a day.

Many people believe that camels store water in their humps. This is not true. The humps are actually large lumps of fat. When a camel is well fed, the animal stores some of its food as fat in its hump. Then, when food is not available, it can live on this reserve source of energy. A camel's hump may contain up to 100 pounds (45.5 kilograms) of fat, allowing the animal to go for many days with no food. When a camel has gone for a long time without eating, its humps become somewhat smaller.

A camel has strong teeth and jaws so it can eat the tough plants that form most of its diet. Sharp cutting and tearing teeth in the front of the mouth are used to break off leaves and twigs. These are then chewed with flat molar teeth in the back.

Like all camels, Mguu was born with six pairs of incisors, or cutting teeth, at the front of his mouth. As a young camel grows older, it will lose the four middle incisors in its upper jaw. A bony ridge will grow in their place. In addition to its incisors, an adult camel has four canine, or tearing, teeth and twenty-two molar, or chewing, teeth.

As it eats, a camel swallows its food almost whole. It can do this because it will chew the food again later. Like other members of the artiodactyl group, camels are ruminants, or cud chewers. The camel's stomach is divided into three parts. When food is first swallowed, it goes to the first stomach, which is called the rumen, where bacteria break down some of the tough plant fibers. The camel then coughs up, or regurgitates, some of the food from the rumen and chews it again. This wad of food is called the cud. After the cud is thoroughly chewed, it is swallowed again and goes to the second and third stomachs to complete the digestive process. This way of eating allows the camel to eat quickly while it is on the move and then digest its food later when it is resting.

Like other camelids, camels have long necks, so they are able to raise their heads to more than 12 feet (3.7 meters) above the ground. This helps them to see for long distances and locate sources of food and water. A camel has good eyesight, and because its eyes are placed on the sides of its head, it is able to see in almost all directions at once. It can see even when the level of light is low, which is useful when grazing at night.

A bony ridge above the eyebrow shades the camel's eyes from the bright desert sun, and long lashes provide protection from blowing sand or snow. Camels also have a third eyelid that comes up from below and covers the eye. This semitransparent lid is useful in a snow- or sandstorm because it allows the camel to protect its eyes but still see where it is going.

Every part of a camel's body helps it to survive in the harsh climate where it lives. Hair, both in and around the ears, gives protection from sun, wind, rain, and snow. The camel also has a good sense of smell and can detect the scent of water from many miles away. Special muscles in its nose allow the animal to open and close its nostrils. If a camel is caught in a storm, it simply closes its nostrils so that nothing can blow into its nose.

The camel's body shape is another adaptation to its environment. Seen from the side, a camel looks huge. However, viewed from the front or back, the camel appears to be tall and thin. When it is cold, the camel can turn its side to the sun and have a great deal of its body warmed; but in hot weather, the camel can face the sun in order to keep most of its body surface away from the direct rays.

As a camel walks, its head bobs up and down and its body moves from side to side in a gentle, swaying motion. The camel's rocking gait is caused by the legs swinging forward one side at a time.

In the wildlife park, Mguu and the other camels amble at a leisurely pace as they move from one feeding area to another. When they become tired, they lie down to rest.

As a camel prepares to lie down, it bends its front legs at the knees and then leans forward until it is kneeling. Then it folds its back legs, also at the knees, and drops to the ground. To stand up, the camel simply reverses this process. When lying down, much of the camel's weight is supported by its chest and knees, which are protected by thick, leathery calluses.

The backs of working camels are usually loaded when the animals are lying down. Camels are strong and can lift heavy loads. Arabian camels can easily carry 500 pounds (227.3 kilograms) or more; the stronger bactrians have been known to carry as much as 1,000 pounds (454.5 kilograms) for short distances. A camel whose load is too heavy or unbalanced will refuse to stand up until its owner adjusts the pack.

Like most of the other animals in the wildlife park, the camels usually rest in the middle of the day. Sometimes they are joined by the tahrs, small sheeplike goats native to the Himalaya mountains in southern Asia. The tahrs seem to think that the backs of the resting camels are small mountains and good for climbing. Usually, if a camel becomes annoyed, it indicates its displeasure by spitting a foul-smelling liquid at the source of the annoyance. Rather remarkably, the park camels didn't seem to mind when the goats climbed on top of them. The camels just continued chewing their cuds.

One reason that camels are so useful as work animals is that they can tolerate a wide range of temperatures. Most mammals must keep their body temperatures more or less constant. If they do not, they may become ill. A camel can change depending on the temperature of the surrounding air. When it is hot, a camel allows its body temperature to go up. Its body temperature may rise from 93 degrees Fahrenheit (33.9 degrees Celsius) at dawn to 105 degrees Fahrenheit (40.6 degrees Celsius) at midafternoon without the camel suffering harmful effects. Then at night when the air temperature drops, the camel's body gradually cools off, using its excess heat to stay warm.

During the cooler winter months, camels are covered with heavy coats. The bactrian's thick winter wool may grow up to 10 inches (25.6 centimeters) long in places, helping to keep the animal very warm. Its dark color absorbs the sun's heat. Arabian camels have less hair and tend to be lighter in color, although they can range from black, gray, brown, and tan to white. In the hotter places where Arabian camels live, a light color helps to reflect the sun's rays.

In the wildlife park, the camels sometimes roll on the ground. The moist earth cools their skin, and the coating of dust on their wool helps to keep out insects.

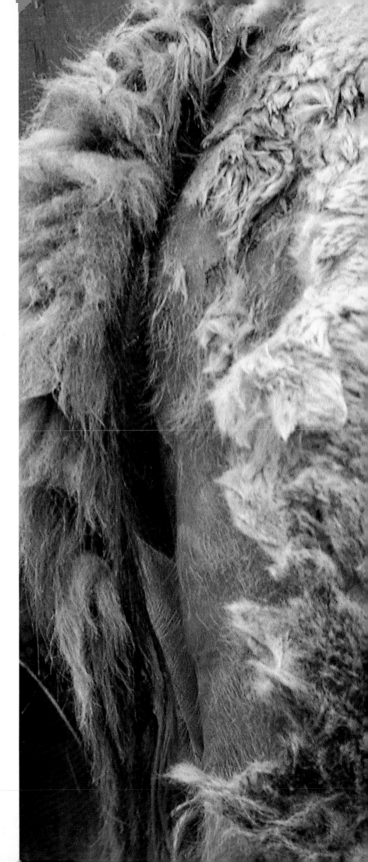

When spring comes, the camels no longer need their heavy winter coats. In a process called molting, their hair falls out in large clumps, revealing sleek new hair underneath. The new hair grows in quickly and helps to protect the camel's skin from the burning rays of the summer sun. The hair is thick again by the time the next winter begins.

For thousands of years people have used camel wool to make tents, blankets, and cloth. The finest camel wool, which is found next to the skin, has a silky quality and is used for clothing. The coarser, outer hairs are made into ropes and rugs. The color "camel" refers to the typical natural tan color of the camel's wool.

By the time Mguu was four months old, he had shed his short, baby wool and was beginning to grow a longer coat like those of the older camels. His face had lengthened and his body was filling out. He now weighed nearly twice as much as he had at birth.

Trina will look after Mguu until he is about four years old. By that time, he will be old enough to be on his own.

Although Mguu will grow rapidly during his first few years, he will not reach his full growth until he is about seventeen. Camels can live for fifty years.

When long, hot summer days dry out the lush spring grass in the wildlife park, Mguu and the other animals have to depend mostly on the feed bins for their food and on the several ponds for drinking water.

When a thirsty camel gets a chance to take a drink, it can consume an enormous amount of water at one time. In hot weather, a camel may drink more than 50 gallons (189.4 liters) of water in one day.

Camels are well adapted to live in dry climates. Many animals, including humans, sweat when they get hot, and the evaporating moisture cools them. Camels, on the other hand, never pant and they do not sweat easily; this helps them to retain valuable body fluids. In addition, the camel's hair absorbs much of the body sweat and helps it to evaporate more slowly. This keeps the camel cooler for a longer period of time. All animals will die if they lose too much water. A person, for instance, cannot live after losing more than 12 percent of the body weight in fluids. But a camel can lose up to 40 percent and still be able to work. Another way that camels retain fluids is by producing highly concentrated urine. Thus, little water is lost when they rid themselves of body wastes.

Camels are amazing animals and are uniquely adapted to live in places where most other creatures could not survive. Although wild camels once roamed over much of the world, there are few truly wild camels left. On the other hand, there are large numbers of domestic camels. Over the centuries, people have developed a special relationship with camels, and in many parts of the world today, camels still provide the most reliable form of transportation. As long as camels are useful to people, they will have a secure place in the world.

Unless you happen to live in a place where camels are part of daily life, your best opportunity to see these unusually shaped animals is at a zoo or wildlife park. As you watch young camels like Mguu grow up there, you can imagine what it might be like to live in a land where food and water are scarce and your life might depend on these sturdy, humped animals. Sometimes called "ships of the desert," camels are among the most interesting and useful animals on earth.

INDEX

Photographs are in **boldface**.